THIS MANIFESTO BELONGS TO

_____

DATE I VOWED TO CHANGE THE WORLD
WITH MY ART

_____

ALSO BY BRANDI AMARA SKYY

Magick For Transformation
Rituals and Alchemy For Manifesting Your Wildest Dreams

Be More Drag
Life Hacks and Tips from the Queens and Kings of the Catwalk

The Little Book of Drag
Divas, Drag Family, Drama, and Deliciousness

Wild Dream Grimoire (Seasonal)
Journaling, Tarot, Moon Rituals, & Other Wild Magick in
Service To Your Wild Dreams

How To Heal The Loss Of A Pet
A Tiny Book About Big Loss

How To Be A Drag Queen
A Guidebook For Female Drag Queens & Emerging Drag Artists

*Plus a plethora of empowering & self-transformational journals at
wokemagicbodega.com/journals*

Collective Learning Magick
Wild Dream Journal Club
Transform your life through the power of journaling & writing

Podcasts
One Minute Sparks For Artivists
The Wild Dream Podcast

The ARTIVIST

A Manifesto & reinforcement of surviving,
thriving, & revolutionizing through the NEXUS
of the humxn experience & intentional
ART MAKING.

by Brandi Amara Skyy

AWAL
PRESS

Published by Woke Magic Press.

For more information or to request usage permission, please address Woke Magic Press, PO Box 1494, Wimberley, TX 78676. Or email the artivist@wokemagic.com

ISBN 979-8-9856699-1-6 (paperback)

Grassroots Edition: January 20, 2025 as an act of resistance to Trump's inauguration.

brandiamaraskyy.com   wokemagic.com brandiamaraskyy.substack.com

Dedication

This book is ...

a love letter to all the humxns that have influenced and inspired my radical heart and rebel mind. Abbie Hoffman. Gloria E. Anzaldúa. bell hooks. Malcolm X. And so many more.

a call to action for all mi gente who are straddling multiple complexities within their singular existence. i see you. *i am you.* May this book be the not needed permission slip that frees you to manifest the art *in* you.

and a gratitude statement to all the spirits that helped me understand that radicalization without hope, that critique without offerings of solution, that either/or extremes and absolutes are not how we will change the world.

Or, at least, not how i'm going to change it.

Caution

Like my art, this book is not for everyone.

Whether or not it's for you, is up to you to decide. To say "yes" or "no, thank you." Either way, the power lies with you.

Learning to work with our own power dynamics and **personal agency*** is the heartbeat of this book.

And this work is not easy. It will test, try, trigger, break, rewire, and reroot you. But …

YOU DO NOT HAVE TO DO IT ALONE.

i am here doing this revolutionary creative work alongside you. And i've created a free Substack community for folks like me/we/us called Wild Dreamers.

You can join me, other Wild Dreamers, and the movement at brandiamaraskyy.substack.com. i also offer many accessible options like the Wild Dream Journal Club to further support you on your creative expressive journey. You can find out more about them in the Resources section located at the back of the manifesto.

If you need help, ask and get help. From me, from other professionals, therapists, your ancestors, your spirit guides, God, Goddess, the Universe, your chosen family, your blood family—whomever you feel most aligned and comfortable with.

At the time of this writing (and most likely forever forward), i'm still in the thick of unlearning and doing the work shared in this book. Still trying to work through all the complexities and the realities of living a life that is rich, joyful, expansive, magickal, fulfilling and just, accessible, artful while also being impactful and allowing myself the grace of being humxn.

It's a lot to ask of one humxn's life. But if not i/we/ us, who? And if not now, when?

i am choosing to answer that question and radical call by sharing the words, ideas, & praxises in this book— however messy it feels and looks like.

By continuing to read The Artivist, you are making the choice to do so as well.

You are choosing your personal agency over someone else's rules, tropes, and beliefs of what is/is not possible.

You are choosing yourself. And that is the most empowered, magickal choice you can make.

To your/our/us forever grand rising.

in lak'ech,
xo-b

Please note: **bolded words** marked with an * are further defined in **Word Artivism** at the end of this manifesto.

Spellcast

More than anything else in our world, art is a universal language. But that language has been monolingual for far too long.

i want this book to change that.

i intend for this book to change that.

But perhaps more than anything, i cast a spell in hopes that this book allows more people of color, ability, queerness, marginalization, and Otherness to unlock the possibility of creative expression—of art—as a means to create change in their lives, their community, and then organically in the world.

May this book be a window into seeing your life as art and a gateway into the reality that you, too, can make art from and out of your life.

Because our experiences, our lineages, our stories are so so rich.

And it's time we cash in on that richness before someone outside us does.

May this book unbind you, your voice, your magick, and your art.

May it be a doorway into being the change you wish to see.

And so it is.

Thank you. Thank you. Thank you.

Table of Contents

3 of Cups: i see you in your most high

i see you in your most high
Here
you are not broken
you have not failed yourself or
your resolutions, intentions, archetypes, or dreams.
You are not a lost cause.

Just as life, social justice, equality, and love
are not lost causes either.
Even though, especially though life can
make it feel that way
when the one we wanted lost
when the scales tip in *their* favor
when we've forgotten or ignored
all that we said we were going to do

In moments of destitution, frustration,
heartbrokeness
anger and disappointment
the light at the end of all our tunnels is,
if we are reading this (and we are all here reading
this),
the most powerful force on our side—
we are all still alive.

Can *you* see you, like i in your most high?

infused with ganas, mixed with spirit, shaken
with agency, and served with love—tough, medicinal,
sweet, pungent, sour,
regardless of flavor

Here, our skins' tastebuds pick up only love.

We got this.
We can do this
together, you & i.
and before you do anything else
i need you to know
We see you in your most high.

We see the divine in you.
We feel the yearning to do something in
your eyes.
We can taste your longing for change, smell your
impatience, and hear your disenchanted cries.

Still, you're alive
And the world sees you in your most high.

This moment right here?
These next four years?
they/we/us are imploring you to rise.

like the Sun
like a paper cut
like a sharp pen
like the Moon
like a monsoon
like a tender tide

Whole, together, as One
we rise to meet our most high.

Intro

"The act of making art exposes a society to itself." Julia Cameron

Art is a revolutionary act.

Art is an act of rebellion.

Art is socio-political commentary.

Not all the time, but it can be.

This is a book about when it "can be" and how we can bring that "can be" into our lives and birth the radical art that is inside us.

And by birth, i mean taking consistent action and finally putting pen to paper, brush to canvas, eye to lens, mouth to microphone, and make our visions a reality.

And by radical art i mean, art that has the potential and power to not only change our lives but the lives of our community—and the world. Art holds a mirror to a society and its people and demands answers, solutions, and justice.

Radical art & artmaking is making flesh the art that *needs* to be born from us.

And the art we as a collective need to experience.

As artists of color, queerness, various abilities, and multiple 'isms'—what i refer to in power, equanimity, and reclamation as "Othered" Artists throughout this book—the most powerful thing we can do for ourselves and our community is to witness, express, and share our ideas, beliefs, and experiences in creative ways. *In artful ways.* In ways that empower us to be channels, portals, and gateways to our own magick, ultimately laying the pathway for others to meet and be theirs.

Because art has the power to change the world.

But even more powerfully, *we* have the power to change our circumstances, our lives, ourselves.

Harnessed together, this creates an unstoppable movement.

Gloria Anzaldúa, the biggest influence in my epistemology and ideological landscape, said, "I change myself. I change the world." And this tiny manifesto you are holding in your hands is a culmination of my research, devotion, and obsession to prove this is so. And to prove once and for all to myself, to you, and the world that despite what anyone says, believes, or tells us to our face or behind our backs our **Otherness IS our power.**

And we have everything we need within us to turn our otherness into powerful art.

Our will is our wand. Our words are our spells. And our art is our medicine—our own unique gift of solution to the revolution.

This book is full of receipts from everyday folxs like you and i who've done extraordinary things with lives labeled ordinary, marginalized, and/or oppressed. Who've changed the world (and their circumstances) by harnessing their Otherness and channeling it into their creative expression and making art as a result.

The Artivist is a movement and manual on how you make it happen for yourself, too.

How you too can see the art that lays dormant in your anger, in your angst, in your restlessness, in your youth, in your age and make something of it. Make something of all those ideas, longings, and yearnings for things that don't yet exist, but you know with every fiber of your being *should* exist. Make something that heals that outlives you and me. And make something of this call to *do something* before we fuck up our world, our society, our culture any more than it already is.

This tome is full of maps of encouragement and processes paired with the tough love and proof i needed to hear and know about when i was first starting out as an artist who wanted to make a difference through their art. It is the memory made flesh of my medicine journey towards a Sacred Warrior and Artivist life.

But it is also a reminder that my creativity is power.

And so is yours.

May this book serve as a guide towards a greater movement of the self. May it inspire you to claim and exclaim your Otherness as your power and galvanize you to create. May it balm your scratches and heal your wounds so as to create the legacy that runs through your blood memories[1].

And may it serve as a reminder that nothing is impossible—not even for us—if you bring your whole self to the table—flaws and all—and share your inner bounty in hope, love, and art.

Thank you for being a part of the solution.

As we speak, create, art; so shall it be.

And so it is.

Thank you. Thank you. Thank you.

---

[1] i first came across the term "Blood Memories" as an undergraduate dance major when we studied Alvin Ailey's work. As far as i know, he is the father of the term which he used to describe, "memories that were so strong that they were part of him, like the blood in his veins." Quote from The Kennedy Center (see resources for more.)

Gateways, Portals, & Keys
My Story

i've always been a creative, expressive, and art-focused person.

i drew, danced, and wrote my way through my childhood, roller-skated and belly danced my way through young adulthood, and dragged my way into full-on witchhood.

And i've *always been* a rebel, a revolutionary, a dissenter. *An Artivist.*

As a baby, i refused to eat beef with my carrots when my mother tried to introduce meat for the first time in my diet #bornvegetarian.

i never learned how to walk. i discovered how to *run.*

In 3rd grade, i was poised to perform Madonna's *Like A Virgin* at our Roman Catholic School's talent show until my father suggested that i choose a different song. i chose Lionel Richie's *Dancing on the Ceiling* instead, invited my neighborhood friend to perform with me, and invoked the ingenuity of my mother to make our costumes—the store-bought basics quickly transformed into couture masterpieces by my mother's hand. The t-shirt became a halter top my mom fringed and beaded at the bottom and the front of the halter became a trail of purple footprints—a stamped pattern my mom had created and carved out of a grocery store potato.

Our grade school cafeteria was transformed into our stage, and i danced my little heart out.

i was 9 years old and had just created my first self-choreographed performance, but my post-stage performance high was met with an angry Sister Mary charging toward me. She grabbed my arm, tighten her grip, and pulled me within an inch of her horned-rimmed glasses and, with fire shooting out of her eyes, whisper-yelled, DON'T YOU EVER DO THAT AGAIN!

i didn't even know what i had *actually* done…dance? Have fun? Expressed myself? Whatever it was, it was forbidden. And that day, thanks to Lionel Richie, i got my first taste of the powerful triggers, emotions, and reactions art can provoke in people, especially if the art in question makes them confront their own biases, values, beliefs, and judgments.

In 7th grade, i did my final history project on the Black Panthers despite my teacher's concerned sentiments of, "Are you sure you don't want to do something else? Are you sure this is for you?"

In the early 90s, in my last few months as an artistic roller skater, a new rule (no sequins or rhinestones on a skater's boot covers) was put into the rulebooks. That same year, i pushed the boundaries of what girls could wear to compete at Nationals when i showed up in a pantsuit. Ultimately i lost the battle (i had to turn my pantsuit into a skirt) but won the war—i showed up in the fullness of me at 15.

But it wasn't until i was 24 that i realized how these two worlds—creativity and speaking and sharing my truth—could merge.

After years of saying i was never going to college, at 24, i finally said yes to it when i learned that i could major in dance. i landed at Texas Women's University in Denton, TX, whose core curriculum required every undergrad student to take an Introduction to Women's Studies course. i took it, and my whole world blew open. TWU's Women's Studies requirement eventually led me to minor in Women's Studies as an undergrad and choose it as my MA degree focus and major.

While the academic world of dance and activism began to swirl around me, in the socio-political world, the U.S. found itself in the middle of destructive and absolutist narratives of "you're either with or against us" patriotism.

Prior to George W. Bush winning his reelection, my then-girlfriend and i had driven over 1,500 miles on a whim to protest Bush and his choice of holding the Republican National Convention in New York after the 911 tragedy. We joined tens of thousands of people who had done the same thing. i was 26 years old, it was my first National protest, and it was a whole other kind of high—the energy was electric, my whole entire soul and body were on fire, and i was using *all of myself and my fire* to make a difference.
We were also there for a deeper, more personal reason.

J, like my father, served in the Army, and with less than a year left in her active reserves duty, she got involuntarily recalled into Operation Iraqi Freedom. We were devastated. Neither one of us believed in Bush's war. Neither one of us had voted for him. Neither of us liked him either. On top of the war and Bush not aligning with our morals and values, Don't Ask Don't Tell was still in full force, and here we were, a gay couple with one partner going off to fight in a war that wasn't ours, and for rights that didn't include us.

It was the first time the political got personal and i consciously felt firsthand the direct effects of Washington politics—and i didn't like it. i felt powerless, out of control, and like there was absolutely *nothing i could do*.

Until i met my anger and frustration with creativity.

Concurrently, i was enrolled in a choreography course that required students to create and choreograph our own pieces. Every time i thought about what kind of dance piece i was going to choreograph, my mind kept skipping to what was happening in my personal life and the question, *What the fuck am i going DO ABOUT IT?*, playing on a forever loop.

The question, *What am i going to do about it?*, became

the flint that my **complex personhood**[2] needed to ignite and invite the spark of creative justice to merge with my artistic vision.

In an instant, *everything changed.* Everything i was experiencing personally and was angry about became a bridge to my creativity and, ultimately, how i expressed it.

Injustice into an idea.

Frustration into formulation.

Disillusionment into dissension.

Angst into art.

Anger into action.

---

[2] i first encountered this term in the essay, "Imagining Differently: The Politics of Listening in a Feminist Classroom" by Sarah J. Cervenak, Karina L. Cespedea, Caridad Souza, and Andrea Strub in the book *this bridge called home* (see Resources). The phrase has nuanced meanings shared in the essay; here is one: "all people . . . remember and forget, are beset by contradiction and recognize and misregonize themselves and others. Complex Personhood means that people suffer graciously and selfishly too, get stuck in the symptoms of their troubles, and also transform themselves."

My lived experienced of the term has taught me that it means this: all experiences, interactions, and things we consume make us who we are at any given moment. That our very essence and nature is complex and therefore expecting anything linear or singular or absolute from any one of us goes against nature's intention and design for us. i use it from the intersection of all it's myriad of definitions in this manifesto.

i marveled at both the choreographical dance concept and story unfolding on the movie screen of my mind and my ability to be a channel and vessel for it. i was floored at the transmutation of all the things i felt— anger, disappointment, fear—into a malleable material i could work with and into my art.

For the first time, The Artivist muse had revealed themself to me and what came of it was the first of many acts of art that led the charge and forged the path of my life lived in service to living, breathing, and becoming an Artivist myself.

And ultimately, offering my way in as a path for the emergence of The Artivist in *you*.

Artivist Notes #1:
How to begin co-co-creating and actioning with this book

The Artivist road you are about to venture down is paved with new concepts, challenging ideas, and words, work, and delivery that will stretch you.

And so before we begin, i want to offer up a few suggestions and words of encouragement.

If you are new to this kind of creative and life exploration, be kind to yourself. The journey towards making art your life, like art itself, is a process of self-discovery. Let it take however long it takes. Make peace with that.

Do not allow doubt, guilt, or shame to stop you from this exploration and your praxis. Instead, get curious about these feelings and ask why they are showing up.

Take it one section, chapter, and sentence at a time.

Take one praxis (see Artivist Note #2 below) exercise (the action you will do at the end of every chapter) at a time and really go deep with it. Let yourself dive as deep as you safely feel you can go. Because what you are doing in each praxis action is building a relationship to your own voice, a solid foundation of your art, and the core of your creative expression. What you do, see, and experience in this praxis work will influence and authenticate your artistry in tangible and holistic ways. Ways that cannot be taught; only learned through first-hand experience.

The deeper you dig and see into the art of your daily life, the more you will be able to outwardly publicly express it—if that's what you decide you want to do.

Finally, the most powerful advice and helpful tip i can give you is one that you probably already have access to—pen and paper. If you can swing a notebook, even better. The binding (or lack thereof) doesn't matter. Just choose an analog place where you can record your discoveries, your thoughts, ideas, words, and whatever comes to you during this time. Make notes.

Lots of notes.

This praxis of keeping a notebook (or what i like to call *An Artivist's Grimoire*) alone will change and charge all aspects of your life.

Your Artivist Grimoire will become one, if not THE, most prized and used tools in your Artivist and Creative Toolkit.

Take radical care in creating, maintaining, and protecting it.

For as you build it, so you build yourself.

Artivists Notes #2:
On The Term Praxis & Praxis Work

If you're new to the term praxis, here's how i explain it in my previous book, *Magick For Transformation: Rituals and alchemy for manifesting your wildest dreams.*

i was first introduced to the term "praxis" as an undergraduate via Brazilian author Paulo Freire's 1968 book, Pedagogy of the Oppressed. *In his work, he defines praxis as "action/reflection" in which he states,*

"It is not enough for people to come together in dialogue in order to gain knowledge of their social reality. They must act together upon their environment in order critically to reflect upon their reality and so transform it through further action and critical reflection." (emphasis mine)

Meaning, praxis is the intersection of theory and the actionizing of that theory, aka the practice of it.

i use the term "praxis" throughout the book because i want you to be an active participant in your creative life. i want you to do the work AND reflect on how doing the work changes you.

Then i want you to go a layer deeper and explore how your personal shifting has/can impact the people and world around you.

This is what i mean when i use the term praxis.

i want us to keep the collective "we" in mind as we work on the singular "me" of creatively expressing ourselves.

Like all my other books, *The Artivist* is a spell and prayer of praxis meaning, the point of this manifesto is not just to read it, but to do it. "It" being doing whatever it takes to bring to life the art inside you.

i know for me there have been plenty of times when i've felt so inspired after reading a book, but the flame quickly died out because i got lost in that "Well, that was great, but what do i do now?" feeling.

These praxis sections are designed to guide you through this phase and help you implement the suggested tools and activities into your real life in a clear way that will hopefully produce profound steps toward making your art—and changing the world.

These are suggestions, prompts, exercises, and points

of praxis to help you deepen into your role as a change-making artist.

Do not skip, skim, or skimp them. They are gateways to help you make your creativity + art manifest.

And will help you create the kind of world you want to live in.

Your first praxis
Name your Gateways

These could also be called *dark nights of the soul* or those moments where you feel you've hit rock bottom because either life happens, you made a bad decision, or systemic racism, genderism, and/or any other 'ism" has made you feel less than your divine birthright.

These stories, events, and/or experiences are also keys to help you unlock your art, creativity, and magick.

You picked up this manifesto either consciously or intuitively because you want to learn more about how to work with the medicine of intersections—specifically the place where art + activism meet.

Taking inventory, and more specifically naming and bringing awareness to those moments in your life, is the first step to not just healing but making art that creates change for the maker and others.

After you name the experience, write down what you did, did not, or maybe wish you did about it. That's where the magick, creative juice, and energy live.

Take a moment now to let your future art take space in your life by setting aside 10 minutes (or however long you have or need) and make a list of your stories and experiences now.

If you're at loss, return to the stories i shared in the *Gateways, Portals, & Keys* chapter in the *Intro* section of this manifesto.

Once you've got a list that feels representative of your journey, grab your Artivist Grimoire and journal through these prompts:

1. What did you learn about yourself, your medicine, your ability to survive and thrive through each of the Gateways you wrote down?

2. Good or bad, positive or negative, just or unjust, for better or worse, how has what you wrote down made you who you are today?

3. If you had to choose one of your Gateways to turn into a piece of art, which would you choose and why?

I. The Artivist: The Call

A holistic glimpse into how we are creatively called to The Artivist life and its expression of it.

One: Spark

Something in us sparks. Comes alive. Jolts the insides of us awake. This jolt makes everything in our world feel more vibrant and electrifying than ever before. It feels like a promise. And tastes like hope.

Sometimes, what inspires this jolt happens from ingesting the powerful art of others. We get lost in a compelling movie, book, or piece of music to the point where it overwhelms us and causes us to question why *we* are not creating things like this with/in our own life.

Sometimes, the jolt is the effect of a culmination of a billion different things happening, a million different experiences being digested and amalgamated within us that just wells up in our bodies and pops into our minds like a hiccup from the depths of somewhere within us.

And sometimes, this jolt springs from an experience, an injustice, or an oppression we face in our day-to-day lives.

More often than not, for those of us who exist on the margins of mainstream society, the ideas that spawn our art *are* rooted in our everyday experiences with society and the world. Something happens—we experience our first brush or slap of inequality; we get called a derogatory name; we witness our people being corralled into fenced quarters, ripped away from their families, children sleeping in foil blankets —and it triggers a fire that rages us to do *something*. To *express* our anger and outrage and create something, anything. A movement. Revolution. Art. *Change.*

But then something begins to happen.

We feel that jolt to act, to do something. And if we are in a safe space, we might explore this expression further by picking up whatever is accessible to us at the time: a pen, a microphone, or our phone. But the exploration is short-lived. And the reality and weight of our marginalized life, the consequences of what we are attempting to do—when we've never seen or had access to someone like us actually doing it—begin to fog over the clarity of that feeling, that spark that led us towards that something we know we must do.

And what happens next is what happens to every other humxn who has ever tried to create something throughout **ourstory***—but with many additional complex layers that we, as marginalized folxs, need to arm ourselves against.

Two: Doubt

We talk ourselves out of it.

Of artion (art + action).

Of exploring further what the jolt jiggled loose inside us.

We talk ourselves out of our idea—*IT'S not good enough.*

We talk ourselves out of our ability to bring the idea to life—*WE are not good enough.*

And instead, we talk ourselves into believing all the things that others, society, our government have said about us, and worse, all the things we have said about ourselves. We begin to compare our faint hint of beginning to the decades-in-the-making body of work of our heroes and peers.

We break down our art before we even get a chance to make it. We talk ourselves out of acting before we have even lifted one foot off the ground.

And then there's the guilt.

The guilt of *wanting* to make art in a culture and society that doesn't value, pay, or reverie artists of color, queerness, or Otherness as much as our white counterparts.

The guilt of choosing something we might see as superfluous as art as a means to change the world.

And the shame of *what if . . .*

What if we *don't make it?* Does it prove the above

right?

What if we *do*? Will the money, fame, and respect mean that you're selling out? And therefore make you and your art unrelatable to the people we began creating it for in the beginning?

And then there's the reality . . .

That art has often been seen as a luxury for our people, especially when met and compared to the necessities and realities of our everyday life.

That there are systems, ideologies, and histories in place that grossly hinder our ability to even find our career "bootstraps"—let alone pull ourselves up from them. (As if bootstraps ever existed in the first place for us Indigenous folxs used to walking barefooted upon the Earth.)

That we cannot *afford*—monetarily, time, energy-wise —to live a life of art.

And what felt like an expansion of the world at the beginning begins to suffocate us under the weight of all the life that makes up our own.

In the face of all this life, it seems impossible to *choose* art.

And yet, so many others of our two-spirited, brothers, sisters, and multi-spirits have been/are doing it.

How?

Three: Agency.

Personal agency*.

A form of choice, but one that understands and respects the complexity and diversity of the humxn spirit and experience.

Because choice, for those of us who have a history of being stripped of it, is a loaded word packed with privilege. But *choice* isn't the end goal we are after.

Choice is but a tool *of* personal agency. It is our personal agency channeled into a single area that results in action, that opens the door for us to *choose*. That's where all these often white, heterosexual, cismale self-help teachers out there get it wrong for us.

It's not the choice to take 100% responsibility for our lives that frees us.

It's taking 100% responsibility for our own *personal agency*. Our own power to create change from within, to manifest and bring about change throughout.

Because while systems in power and lawmakers who hide under the guise of inclusivity and "our best interests" may try to strip us of our right to choose— womxn from the right to decide what happens to their own body; what gender we can be or marry; who we elect to offices via gerrymandering, illegal redistricting, and Russian interference; who our lands *really* belong to, along with the ourstory of who

Columbus *really was*—they can NEVER strip away the ways in which we empower and invoke our personal agency and *produce* + *respond*. Creating movements, humxn barricades, taking the streets, organizing the resistance, taking to social media, and making art that speaks the truth. Our truth.

Personal agency is the source of all our power.

And our gente who are making art despite and within all the circumstances that would pressure them otherwise, do it from the center where personal agency, anger, and urgency meet. They are able to do this because they are rooted in something more powerful than ego, capitalism, or the injustices they face. *They are rooted in belief.*

Belief in themselves.

Belief in their own power.

Belief in their ability, through the currency of personal agency, to be the change.

And then they set out to do it. They make that mixtape and distribute it around town. They pick up a pen and draft their first Op-Ed. They grab their phones and start snapping photos of the resistance.

They grab whatever they can find, and they set out to do—to make shit happen for themselves, on their own terms.

And this, mi gente hermosa, is exactly what i am asking, imploring, empowering you to do through this manifesto. i am asking you to take a risk. To do the work you are being called, pulled, jolted to do. To make a priority the things that no one will pay you for, that you will find no applause for in the beginning.

To combat all the additional layers of obstacles, access, and privilege you face as an Othered Artist trying to make it as an artistic and revolutionary force and voice in this world.

To bet on yourself. To bet on your vision for the world.

And to invest in your personal agency. Invest in your voice.

And to believe, with every fiber of your being, that you and your art can be the change you wish to see—and that others need you to be.

Praxis:

Grab paper, your computer, your notebook, phone, whatever is accessible, and answer the following Artivist Shadow Work inquiries.

1. When have you felt the kindling of the spark and jolt and what happened after? (Did you follow it? Did you ignore it? What did you do instead? Did you try to distract yourself by scrolling on Instagram, binging Netflix, etc.?

Think about what went down after you felt that initial pull to create.)

2. When, why, and where have you stopped or sold yourself short?

3. When have you caved to other people's definition of who you are and who you can be?

4. What do you believe about your personal agency and choice?

5. What role does doubt play in your life, dreams, and creativity?

6. What do you believe is truly so impossible for you to do that you won't even try?

7. When have you betted against yourself? More importantly, *what are you going to do about it NOW?*

II. The Artivist: How & Where To Begin

So now that you/i/we/us have a better understanding of what happens when we feel the call to make art as a means of (and to) change, how do *we* begin?

How do we *do?*

How do we make sense of all the chaos, the Pandora's Box we've opened by choosing to use art as our tool for self-expression, self-transformation, and our ofrenda for societal change?

What is the first step in turning what we are feeling, experiencing, and expressing into something that feels like art?

The answer is, has always been, and will always be— **we start where we are with what we have.** And our gateway, our entry point into *living* this is becoming hyper-aware of what is already available, present, and accessible all around us. How?

Intention and *attention.*

We begin to see our everyday tools--our phone, laptop, headphones, pen, and paper in new extraordinary ways. We start to witness the art, and all the things that can *become* art, that *already* surround us—a blank piece of paper, our voice memos, leaves, magazines, crayons, our social media, our body, a pine cone. And get comfortable seeing and calling all these things tools and pathways to *art*.

This innovation and reimaging of our tools and the things that surround us is itself making art.

We also have to shift our own perceptions and definitions of what constitutes as art—as well as any stigmas, expectations, or rules as to how it can be created. It helps to understand that art, like beauty and magick (and really everything in life), is in the eye of the beholder and no two beings will ever see or experience something in the same way as well as reminding ourselves that what is often attributed, constitutes, and is 'valued' as art is often defined by a privileged, self-appointed few based on societal, colonized, and hetero-European standards.

One of the ways that i began to shift my definitions and perspectives of art was by reclaiming the art of my ancestors, the art that was *already* in my blood memories.

The art that is inseparatable us.

The art that has been with me/we/us since birth.

The art that mainstream society and culture label folk or exotic.

And the art that is often labeled, even by us, as *homemade* automatically seems to lend itself to an art form that is less desirable or valuable than others, particularly since society as a whole tends to view home life and work as less useful since others cannot capitalize upon it.

But as Artivists, we know better.

We know that when we strip art of all its quantifiers what we are left with is simply art.

And art is a spell that can be found any and everywhere.

Here's an example from my life.

When, against all odds and his family's wishes, my father graduated with his Bachelor's in 1984 my mother threw him a dance at the Elk's Lodge. We went to Dillards in the Sunrise Mall to find a suit for him. While they were searching, i ended up finding the *perfect* party dress that made me feel like a princess. i fell in LOVE with its baby blue satin floor-length empire waist design; its white lace ruffle accents and its puffed capped sleeves. It was the most beautiful dress my 6-year-old eyes had ever seen. It looked like Cinderella's ball gown come to life. And i wanted it.

But it was also waaaay out of our price range—in fact, the entire store was! i left the store disenchanted and empty-handed. Little did i know that i too, like Cinderella, had my own fairy godmother.

A few days before the party, my mother surprised me

with the dress!

Only it wasn't the dress from the store. It was a dress that *she* made. An almost *exact* replication but with touches she knew i would love that the original dress didn't have: iridescent sparkle ruffled lace that trimmed the collar and the sleeves. She sewed the same ruffles on my socks. Gave the dress diamond buttons!

i remember this dress and moment, not because i got the expensive one from the boujie department store, but because my mother, through her own creative and artistic ingenuity, with the gift of her own artist's hands, made my dream of wearing that dress at my dad's graduation party a reality.

i will forever remember that dress because my mother had found a way to make something beautiful, magical, and unforgettable out of our nothing. And because my mother had wielded her hands as her wands and made me wearable art.

And despite never being on the cover of *Vogue* or having a fancy atelier in Paris, *my mother was/is a couturier.*

The very definition of couture—the kind that celebrities pay outrageous prices for—is handmade garments made to one's specific standards and measurements. And my mother—and so many other mothers, fathers, and parental figures—*do that* for their kids. Beyonce's mother immediately comes to mind as she made everything for Destiny's Child.

But it wasn't until i was in my late 30's that i understood and *recognized* my homemade clothing as the art of couture. In fact, i had been wearing couture my entire young adult life—from my school clothing to the skating costumes i would design and my mom would make. But i never valued it as such because my hand and homemade clothing was birthed from necessity, not opulence, and was not what others like Anna Wintour and other fashion editors, movies, and mainstream culture sold and taught me/we/us was couture.

But it is.

And as Artivists, it's time to start claiming it as such.

These kinds of creations and creation stories, these ingenious moments, are what i mean when i i say, *we need to start where we are and reclaim our own personal ancestral art*. Because these moments and experiences right here? These are moments of *real, authentic, life-altering art*.

And ultimately, art's purpose is to inspire deep transformation, recalibration, shifts, and change—the kind that leaves us breathless because it causes us to undergo the entire range of emotions in a split-second period, brings tears to our eyes, and wakes up every cell in our body to pulsate in unison to *this moment right here*.

Moments where art moves us, our lives, our stories, and our creations forward (which *is exactly* what art is meant to do) provide and help us *progress*.

This *is the meaning of life*.

And art helps us get there.

Art gets us closer to the infinite divine. To God. Goddess. The Universe. The force that animates all things.

That's what art does.

My mother's blue satin dress did that for me.

And i know you've felt those infinite, divine, and powerful art moments too.

Our lives are filled with them. Filled with tiny unseen, unlabeled, taken-for-granted moments of art because we haven't been indoctrinated and trained to see them, *value them*, and name and claim them as "Art."

It's a small shift that leads to profound, lasting change. First, in ourselves, and ultimately the world through what we create.

So our job now as Artivists is to decolonize ourselves, deprogram our understanding of art, and begin to see, define, and create art in new unprivileged and unbiased ways.

Our job is to see the art that surrounds us, that we bypass, overlook, or disassociate from the word because it's been labeled common, uninteresting, normal, everyday, folk, or homemade, and reclaim them as the art that they intrinsically are.

Rap. Graffiti. Car wrapping. Wig and hair art. Drag. These are just some of the many art forms rooted in culture or counter-culture that haven't always been labeled or viewed as art *even though they are.* Or they become labeled as art via mainstream pop culture when someone outside the original culture sources and appropriates them—and then a magazine calls them the latest trend. Or they've won an Emmy, Grammy, or some other 'academy' that deems them worthy.

But we are surrounded by art-making every day.

Baristas who take the time to craft intricate patterns out of the foam on the top of mochas and cappuccinos. They are artists.

Our abuelitas carefully kneading masa into tufts that look like mushroom tops to then roll them out into perfect tortilla circles. They are artists.

Or mothers alchemizing spices of thyme and other Jamaican seasonings to spread over our rice and peas. They are culinary artists just as worthy of Michelin stars.

The turning of the Medicine Wheel and leaves

changing from seed, bud, and flower; green, lime, brown. This is art.

And our mother/grandmother/father/**mapas*** who made our clothes growing up because they couldn't afford 'designer' were couturiers. All were and are artists.

These seemingly mundane daily acts are Art—with a Capital A. Our life is filled with Art. We just need to recognize, acknowledge, and value it as such.

And as we continue to pour our attention and awareness into the nuances in our daily life, our own connection to art grows stronger. The longer we use our personal agency to ultimately define what art is, we strip the power and policing of art's borders out of *their* hands and bring them back into our own.

We remind ourselves that not all art can be found in bookstores, heard on the radio, or be seen hanging in the Louvre. And ultimately, art is more about belief, feeling, and the intentionality behind it than the applause it garners.

And so gente, we cycle back to the beginning and the question that got us here.

How do we begin?

We begin now. With the most potent powerful tool at our command—our personal agency. With our eyes, hearts, and fists wide open to experiencing and seeing our life in a whole new artistic way.

And we start this adventure into art by *doing.* By actionizing ourselves.

The praxis below is a beautiful place to start.

Praxis

For this praxis section, you will focus on remembering and reclaiming your art and witnessing the artistry of the world around you—and your own life.

i suggest reading through the entire praxis first and then feel into which one feels most potent. Intuitively decide. Start there. And give yourself room to explore. Don't try to rush through it all in one day. Time is a humxn-made concept and you are not running out of it.

Grab your Artivist Grimoire and begin.

1. Like the story of the blue satin dress my mother made me, look back at the events and experiences that make up your life and start to curate and collect the stories of art that appear throughout it.

   If you do not have access to stories that include parents, guardians, or siblings, you have access to yourself.

Think back to moments in your life when *you* got creative and unknowingly made art out of your experience. If you need some real-life examples, head over to the *Further Exploration/Resources* section at the back of this manifesto.

2. As you walk down the street or take the bus or subway to work, keep all your senses open as you venture into your day to look for random acts or displays of art.

3. Start paying attention. Real attention. Focused attention. That means get off your phone and become an active participant in your own life. Watch your bartender craft your cocktail. Witness the choreography your mechanic does when they change the oil in your car. Watch how your hands dance as they create words on the page. Notice nature's organic artistry of colors, ombres, and textures.

   Make note of how your attention shifts and changes the thing you are observing. Keep track of what you find most inspiring.

4. The following praxis is based on one of my favorite writers, Dani Shapiro, daily quadrant writing exercises. i have tweaked it to make it more Artivist specific.

- Divide a piece of paper into 4 quadrants.
- On the top left side, write the word, *Saw*.
- On the top right side, write the word *Did*.
- On the bottom left side, write the word *Heard*.
- On the bottom right side, write the word *Express*.

Then list out 7 things you "Saw" today that said 'art' to you. 7 things you "Did" that could be considered art (by you and no one else's standards). 1 thing you "Heard" that felt like art (could be a sentence, a sound, a vibration). Then, "Express" can either be a doodle, poem, photo, collage, or whatever you feel called to create about something on your list.

As Dani states, this helps us to curate our inner observer—the person we need to be to write (or create any kind of art) well.

i've been doing this praxis for the last 7 years, and it has really opened me up to the magick of the daily mundane.

Also, feel free to make it your own and/or substitute out different senses. Maybe do taste vs. heard or smell vs. seeing. Again, when we get artful with our lives, then we invite art deeper into it.

A final note about this praxis: "Saw" and "Heard" are not linked with the physical ability and sense of sight or hearing. Folxs "see" and 'hear" in a myriad of ways. You do not need to be able-bodied to tap into this praxis.

5. One of my art (and lifesaving) tools i keep near me as i set forth on new artistic adventures is what i call *My Proof Of What Is Possible* list. This is a curated list of all the things i've done in my life that others have deemed impossible—like being a USofA pageant-winning drag queen (and a drag queen in general), getting published in major media outlets (*BET* and *Curve Magazine*) to the small things like making a living off my art, quitting my 9 to 5 to go my own art way, and healing my body.

You can do hard, impossible-to-most-people things. And you *have already done hard, impossible things.*

Take a moment in your Artist Grimoire to list all the things you've done that folxs told you were impossible.

You might want to take a snap of the list and keep it on your phone for quick and easy access. You also might want to print it out and put it up where you can see it wherever you do your creative and Artivist work.

6. Answer these inquiries in your Artivist Grimoire.

    1. What is your personal definition of art? This book is the modus operandi of mine.
    2. What are some of the things in life that you have always seen or believed were art, but that others—be it mainstream, the art police, your friends, or family—have told you were not?
    3. What do you want to say with and/or inspire others to be/do with your art?

You don't have to know all the answers to these questions or do all the praxis work in this first section to move forward. Just get some ideas down and trust yourself to know when you're ready to move on.

Remember, art is progress. Art is movement.

In the spirit of Art, *keep on pressing forward.*

III. The Artivist: Turning Our Experiences Into Art

By redeeming your most painful experiences you transform them into something valuable, algo para compartir or share with others so they too may be empowered - Gloria E. Anzaldúa

In the last chapter, we began to reclaim ourselves as Artists, Artivists, and the Art that has always been present in our lives.

As you were going through the praxis work, you might have felt something—an idea, an experience— light up. And light you up. It might have been as bold as a spotlight on a specific project or as a soft shimmer that felt like potential and possibility.

Or . . . maybe it felt like a punch in the gut with a steady (or fast) stream of anger.

Whatever kind of bodily reaction you had is valid. Having no bodily response is also valid.
But as someone who has repeatedly gone through the praxis work above over and over again, i'm willing to bet that you felt *something*.

Because that same *something* called you to pick up this manifesto, and we're not looking for a specific kind of reaction; we are just looking for a reaction, *period*. Because it is those elements, ideas, experiences, and moments that *spark* a response in us—whether it's anger, desire, hope, or curiosity—that call us to make art out of them. Or, at the very least, explore the possibility of it becoming art.

When i was first trying to uncover what would eventually become the choreography of *Beating Around The Bush* (the story i shared at the end of *Gateways, Portals, & Keys*), i had *NO idea* what i wanted to do or what i wanted to say. But the events that were happening in my life at that time and my reaction (anger, disbelief) to the things in it—inequality, unrealistic beauty standards, privilege, my girlfriend going off to fight in a war for a country that wouldn't allow us to get married or even notify me if anything were to happen to her—sparked the embers of an idea which led to the flame of a tangible concept that i could use as a base point to start building and creating upon.

The truth of radical art-making is that the experiences that provoke a reaction in you *that trigger you* are the spaces and places where your art wants to take root. Art is a pathway to healing. Our emotions are barometers of how far we've come—and how much further we still need to go.

And so the first step in our endeavor towards art-making—where we take an intangible idea and turn it into something tangible and of this world—is to recognize that our experiences, emotions, and reactions to the events and situations in and of our life *want to be* expressed; need to be expelled; and want to be made something of.

We are all expressive creatures by nature. And we are constantly in a state of expressing ourselves—even if we are not conscious of it.

Art turns our expression conscious.

And so the next step in our Artivist making is to turn our feelings, emotions, and experiences into conscious expression through the act of *self-expression*, i.e. creativity, i.e., through the making of something.

And this is where it gets a bit hazy—and where most folxs get stuck and/or give up because the process of turning your experiences, emotions, and ideas into art is a deeply personal and alchemical act—one that *no one* can dictate for you. You can invoke guides like this manifesto, but ultimately, you will only find your Art by doing it. By trial and error. Trying and failing. Practicing and doing. Over and over again.

But here's the good news.

You've already been doing it. You've already been making art from your life.

The praxis work in the previous section, where you combed through your past to uncover the art in it, is a form of turning your experiences into art. You are taking an otherwise uneventful moment in your personal history and reframing, reshaping it, and molding it into something else—art.

When you did the quad exercise in your Artivist

Grimoire, you were taking things you were seeing, doing, or experiencing in the now and turning it into art. That doodle, mini poem, or photo you might have seen as a throwaway act of creation is a piece of art that was not in this world before YOU picked up a pen and drew it into being.

But it's not just in this book's praxis work where you can find proof of you turning your experiences into art; chances are *you've been doing it all your life*—you just weren't conscious that THAT was what you were doing.

Here are some examples of what i mean.

Have you ever felt a strong emotion like anger or love and reached for your phone to find the perfect song that expresses, amplifies, or decompresses your mood and hit play? THAT is taking your emotions and finding a way to express them via art.

Have you ever sought out a movie or binge-watched a series on Netflix to match (or contradict) whatever it is you're feeling at the moment—sad, happy, inspired? THAT is turning the feelings you experience into art. And/or attempting to change them.

Have you ever felt so shook or angry that you just had to jump in your car and drive? THAT is you trying to move, action, and *express* the feelings out of you.

The root of the word expression is expression is express—which means to squeeze or expel something out of a thing, in this case, that thing is you.

And that's what art is—an ***express***ion of our emotions, thoughts, and experiences into tangible form.

In the examples above, you/i/we/us expressed ourselves through other people's art. But what if we made one tiny shift from outside to in?

What if instead of reaching for Spotify to listen to someone else's expression of the emotion you are feeling, you hit record and verbalized/sang out what you were going through? Or grabbed a piece of paper and started spitting out lyrics?

What if instead of clicking on Netflix, you picked up a phone and made a mini-movie of your own? Or took a few photos of things that mirror how you are feeling—or perhaps what you *want* to feel.

What if instead of getting into your car and driving to move out the energy, you danced it out? Or belted it out in a sing-song of words as they come to you?

What if instead of reaching for already produced pieces of art, you turned that energy inward and created your own?

THIS, my beautiful familia, is what art-making looks like. This is what being an Artivist looks like on a daily.

And this is how accessible it can be to turn your experiences into art.

Starting here, with small little substitutions of other people's art for your own, is enough to get you arting for the long haul. This. Is. How. We. Begin. These are the small steps that become giant leaps in our creative, magical, Artivist future.

This is how we use ourselves and our experience to begin to change the world.

Praxis

There is only one praxis work for this section: to begin to play with expressing your emotions/ experiences as art instead of turning to other people's art to do it for you. Remember that these don't have to be big and grand expressions—tiny expressions are just as impactful as large ones.

Here are a few suggestions to help guide you through this experiment.

1. For the next week, watch for moments where you organically reach for something—the radio, television, social media, a book—to help you outwardly express what you're feeling.

    When you observe this happening, acknowledge it and then pick up whatever tool feels right to you—a paintbrush, computer, pen and paper, camera, or phone —and try to emote and express (remember: squeeze out of you) what you are feeling in your own words and way.

2. Pay attention to your emotions as you go through your day. Maybe you read an article or post on social media that riles you up. Maybe it's something on the news. Take all that energy and anger and *use it*. Funnel it into poetry, a drawing, or perhaps an article of your own.

   One of my mentors calls this writing from the heat—writing (and in this case, creating) from the center of hot, riled-up feelings of pissed-the-fuck-off-ness.

3. Think about the kind of art you want to create long-term. Now, pick one of the moments you reclaimed as art in the previous section's praxis and experiment with how you can turn it into your chosen modality of art right *now*.

   For example, using the story of my blue dress: If i was going to make art of it now in the form i feel most called to (writing), i could craft that moment into a short story, or personal essay, or the beginning of a novel or memoir.

If i wanted to be a visual artist, i could paint, draw, or collage the dress.

If i wanted to be a photographer, i could snap photos of things that were baby blue or channel the feelings of the moment i saw and put on the dress.

If i wanted to be a poet, i could craft it into a poem. A singer, craft it into lyrics. A fashion designer, sketch and make a modern-day version of my baby blue Cinderella dress.

The possibilities are endless.

Just choose the possibility that feels right for you now, and begin.

Artivist Notes #3:
You could and can stop here

Alright familia, here's what i want you to know before moving forward.

You could stop reading this manifesto at the end of this sentence and call yourself an artist and Artivist.

Everything you've been doing and exploring in the praxis work until now is enough to claim it. Even half is enough. Even one slight movement towards living a more aware life is enough.

It all counts. It's ALL enough.

Because the depth, intentionality, and focus you are now bringing into your life *is* the mastery skill of any kind of artist. And it's truly where art begins and continues to live.

A songwriter writes about the world they see and experience daily—and perhaps the world they Imagine it can be.

An artist paints or draws what they can see—figuratively, relatively, or metaphysically.

A photographer captures the nuances and complexities of a multi-dimensional life in a single frame.

And a writer writes in homage to the imaginary wonderland inside them.

All artists create their art in a silo of themselves. The result of expelling what is inside us is art and a form of activism before anyone else sees, reads, or touches it because art happens and still means something regardless of anyone watching or clapping.

And i want to share the importance of this because i really want you to unlearn the idea that art has to be consumed by a plethora of others to be considered "real art." Art happens regardless if only your mother reads your books or 50,000,000 million strangers do.

You do not have to go any further in this exploration than you already have to live as an Artivist. What you've read and been doing thus far is more than enough to change the course of your life—and inspire change in the folxs who bear witness to the intentionality in which you are now living your life.

If you find and feel that this space is enough, stay here. If you want to linger in the decolonizing, unlearning, and reclaiming of your inner Artivist voice, keep meandering. Know that it's okay to swim in these new open waters for as long as it feels right and good for you.

You have permission to be an Artivist and make art on a strictly personal level. IT IS ENOUGH. Period.

But/and/also/all . . .

For those of us who feel the call of The Artivist beyond the personal (and you'll know if this is you because you'll feel a stirring and kindling in your gut —like a wild animal rustling out of hibernation), the following sections in this manifesto will help you make art your life's work and bring the personal into the public—and, if you so chose, into the political.

IV. The Artivist: Public Arting

Up until this point, we've been creating for ourselves.

How do we move beyond that? How do we take what we've been making and share it with the world to create an impact?

Again, the answer is simpler than we think: We start small and don't wait for our art to be perfect.

"Perfectionism is the voice of the oppressor, the enemy of the people."

i have these words by Anne Lamott on a Post-it note above my writing desk. It serves as a reminder that i WILL NOT police myself by buying into this capitalist and patriarchal notion of "perfect."

We resist by sharing our Art *as is*. With close friends, a writing coven, on social media, a mentor, on our blog, Substack—whatever public arena we have access to and feels good for us. We share it in whatever form it wants to be shared in—fully edited, crafted, and curated or as a work in raw progress.

We don't worry about getting it "right"—there is no "right" or "wrong," no absolutes, in creative expression and Artivism.

We don't worry that others may not see or call our work "art"—the only person's voice we need to care about is our own.

The only things we should concern ourselves with right now are why we feel called to share and what and where we are going to share. Knowing our purpose and why we feel pulled to share will engender our courage and amplify our bravery.

Still . . .

Sharing is hard. It might be, in my opinion, the *hardest* part. Because with sharing comes a whole new slew of emotions, limiting beliefs to unpack, and past personal experiences and/or traumas to face.

Sharing *is* shadow work because it forces us to bring to light (as we bring our art to the spotlight) all the pieces and parts of us that are the most tender, vulnerable, and scary.

Sharing our art—especially when it is infused with our personal experiences, marginalizations, trials, and tribulations—can feel like a deep vulnerability cut that won't heal, and every time we share our work, it feels like the wound is being forced open again and again. Making us even *more* vulnerable to being hurt, marginalized, oppressed, chastised, ostracized, and/or Othered even more than we already were and/or are.

But all evolution, all revolution, requires a vulnerable openness to life.

This radical vulnerability—this unabated, unrelenting, deep empathy for justice, love, and equality for all—

compels the revolutionary forward. Choosing to care enough to act—the essence of an activist—takes courageous vulnerability and exposure to all the elements: people's rising temperatures, political polarities, and stripped-away rights.

It's knowing all this, feeling scared, and sharing anyway.

And courageously sharing is the portal in which your art, and you as an Artivist, will break through. Radical vulnerability and courageous sharing will be the current that propels your art forward from private to public.

Here's what i know to be true: The first share is always the hardest.

But the more you do it, the less scary it gets. The more you step into your own creative power, the more revolutionary you become.

And the more you do that, the more familiar it becomes to your heart and nervous system, making each share a little less shock-inducing and a little more *easeful*, not easy. It will never be easy for folxs like us. But we *have to do it anyway. This* is what unlearning, deprogramming, and rewiring ourselves looks like—the same action taken again and again until it becomes our new norm.

And reorienting ourselves towards a more self-expressive and expansive art-as-part-of-the-solution is the sole and soul intention and spellcast of this manifesto.

In our self-reclamation and self-reorganization, we learn new things about ourselves while unlearning all the humxn-made beliefs that have stunted our personal and collective creative and spiritual growth.

Therefore, we make our private acts of art public by sharing them, and by sharing them, we stretch and repattern ourselves.

But/and/also/all . . .

We share so that others like us feel represented, empowered, and free to do so as well.

Make sharing your work, in all its stages—from beginning to process to completion—a ritual, part of your daily creative and spiritual hygiene routine.

What becomes of this habit, of your consistent doing, of you going first, is that you begin to erode the mountain of impossibility that everyone else was too afraid to climb. You pioneer your own path while leaving a map of footprints for *your gente* to follow and refuel in the form of artistic breadcrumbs.

Every time you take a step towards sharing your work, that mountain of impossibility gets smaller and smaller. Every time the soul of your foot brushes the terrain, you pave the way for others. And *you become the proof of possibility that you originally were seeking*.

You become *The Artivist*.

And by walking your own path, you organically become a steward, a guide, a leader for others.

Show us how you got there so that i/we/us can replicate it.

Share your stories so we may use them as medicine and balms as we navigate through the growing pains of creating our own way in a society and world that continues to show us how unjust and hateful humxnkind can be.

Share your visions for the kind of world you want to live in, the world you are creating through your art. What does it look like? What does it feel like? What solutions do you all bring to the table? What role does your art play in the solution? How can we get in on *your movement?*

Share. Share. And share some more.

This is how The Artivist is born: out of necessity, out of our own experiences, out of the need to do something with our stored-up energy, anger, frustration, and heartbreak, and out of the connective medicine of sharing.

Sharing connects us to those people, places, and things the world tries to separate us from.

Sharing heals the self while helping others see the

fissures in themselves that need healing.

Sharing, like i did with this manifesto, connects me to you, and you, in whatever creativity this book fosters in you, to me.

Sharing cycles us back into the revolutionary truth that we are stronger together than we are apart.

As you channel, create, and share your art, you are now a contributor in the most powerful role of life—that of creatrix, artist, and healer.

To be an Artivist means to do all of this—from saying yes to the spark of an idea to alchemizing our experiences to public arting to sharing—*on purpose.*

Let us begin.

Praxis

Your praxis for this section is to share your work. *Today. Tomorrow. The next day. And the next.*

Stretch yourself even more by devoting time each day to share your work publicly. You can create a sharing calendar or you could just fly off the cuff.

Or you could do a mixture of both.
Whatever you decide, keep showing up. Keep sharing.

And above all else, keep connecting. To yourself. To your art. To your gente. To your hut (heart + gut). Your art to the world.

And the world back into your (he)art.

V. The Artivist: Doing It All On Purpose

Our otherness IS our power.

And when we harness our otherness into powerful art, then art becomes a tool for radical transformation and (r)evolution—for ourselves and the world.

That is the soul of The Artivist—creation not just for ego and bloodlines sake but for the advancement, liberation, and sovereignty of the people. Their people. Our people. One love all people.

And liberation for *our/themselves.*

The only difference between someone who arts on purpose and any of us is that The Artivist is self-aware enough to know that their work, art, and what they do everyday has the power to impact everything and all. And they also take conscious steps towards crafting a body of work and life that can reach beyond their own healing.

They know that self-knowledge and **radical personal alchemy*** is a revolutionary act and they continue to do the self-work *even when it's charged with discomfort.*

They understand their power lies in what makes them different, and they cultivate that difference and channel it into creating shit that makes the universe, themselves, and their gente proud.

They operate under the wholehearted belief that their expression and art are what they give back to the world as an agent and bearer of change.

Each and every one of us—the woke, awakening, and rising—has the power to do this too.

But we must first radically believe and then consistently embody and praxis this one life and course-altering belief: **Our Otherness IS our power**. And all the Otherness that society, politicians, systems, and the government use as weapons against us are, first and foremost, the tools that can change us.

And change the world.

And can lead to one-of-a-kind art making and solution-oriented self-expression.

That's the work of The Artivist.

And if you've been doing the praxis work as you made your way through this book, then you have *already been* doing Artivist work because Artivism is the bloodline and spine of this manifesto.

Now and forever, your only job is to start to shift your sights back onto that powerful truth: **that you are**

an agent of change and your art is a portal of possibility and transformation.

And be the embodiment of that truth every. single. day.

Because what we create on a daily basis via the art of our life has the power to change everything.

What we create on canvas, on the page, in movement, or on the mic has the power to transform everything.

YOU have the power and personal agency to change YOU. And therefore, the world.

Change yourself, change the world.

As an Artivist, i live and will die by this creed. It's the soul energy powering this manifesto and my personal movement that propels every single one of my creative projects forward.

As an Artivist, you must find yours.

You must find that movement, mission, and creed you'd be willing to put everything on the line for.

And make no mistake, life, politicians, systemic 'isms,' social media, hateful humxns—the whole underbelly of life, will demand you do.

Change will always demand this kind of devotion.

As Artivists, we put ourselves on the line with our voice and body every time we take to the streets, lobby politicians, dissent, or vote. As consumers, we do this every time we choose to purchase something from a particular store, person, or environment. And as spiritual beings having a humxn experience, we do this by continuing to choose to be here despite our circumstances, despite the shit hitting the fan, despite Trump, the Supreme Court, and either extreme.

And by continuing to say yes to doing the work of a changemaker. Of a revolutionary. Of an Artivist.

This is not everyone's calling.

But it is mine. And it is yours too—otherwise, you wouldn't have picked up this manifesto.

It's not easy. It will *never be easy.*

But that's why we create. To express some of the pressure off ourselves. To make the journey to inclusivity, equality, and justice for all just a little more rooted in beauty, love, and art than empty anger and violent hate. And because through our creations, we are molding and shaping the narrative into *the change we wish to see.*

We are shaping our own change, and stories, and creating our own arches every time we choose the pen, microphone, or canvas over the easier more accessible tool of hate.

Put your expression (art) where your marginalization is.

That is how we change the world with who are and what we have access to right now.

Every morning, as i step into the day's work, i am choosing to put my most powerful tool at my disposal —my personal agency—into areas of myself that others label marginalized. And to transmute all that gunk into art that holds the potent medicine of change.

You can choose this pathway too.

You've already chosen it.

Now, you just have to show up for it.

This next praxis work is one more opportunity to do so.

Praxis

Find your movement, mission, and creed.

This praxis work might just be the most important work you do outside of regular, consistent, creative action.

But even action requires deeply understanding one's heat, passion and movement, and creed. This is why, if you don't intimately know yours by now, it's time to recover, discover, and unleash it. The following praxis work will help you dig into the how.

Questions for the revolution:

1. What are some of the things, laws, structures, institutions, and beliefs that rile you up, get you pissed off, and heated to get up and *do* something? Why do these things make you feel this way?

2. What change-making work have you already done or felt called to? (Have you marched in a protest? Written an op-ed? What actions have you already taken and what was the cause behind your fire?)

3. What causes have you always felt intuitively drawn to? Or…What cause, situation, or event—in your life or in our world—drew you to this manifesto?

In the process of asking and answering these questions, your body will build up a lot of heat. *Pay attention to that.* Where does your fire organically rise? That's a clue into what moves you.

And honestly? i believe you already know—just like i did.

Whenever i'd ask myself these kinds of questions, i would rack my brain to logic my way to the answers, those answers that my mind felt were "right." And yes, my logical answers *were* a reflection of me and my movement and therefore very much true, but they lacked the one thing we need to do this work on a continual, forever basis: *heart.*

Were the answers i logically came up with a good place to start? Absolutely. And if this is where you're at, it's good enough to hit go . . . and GO!

But the only path we can ever sustain—and will ever sustain us—is the one with heart. The one that resides in our blood memories, blood lines, and blood wounds.

And where my logic would see and list all the causes i deeply care and fight for in fragments, dualities, and the illusion of separation—us vs. them; this or that—or in the perception of things, solutions that have already been done, my heart could, can, and does innovate a totally different way.

A way where joy, art, and magick are more than just part of the equation—they are THE big, necessary components for the solution.

So, as you begin to shift through your answers, ask yourself: *Does this path have heart?*

Does this path have *my* heart? **Does this path hold my sacred flame?** Or is my path and flame being fanned and fueled by the hate of others—society, politics, the media?

What i have discovered after decades of undergoing

this very same praxis process and constantly asking and answering these questions for myself is my movement and creed will always align with my core values and unshakable beliefs:

We are all connected.

None of us are free until we are all free. And by all i MEAN ALL—humxns, animals, birds, the environment, Earth.

This is radical thinking—an ALL freed from hierarchy, a class system, murder, or separation. It's also a hard sell for most humxn-centric folxs. But/and/also/all it is the path with the most heart *for me.*

What is the path with the most for you, i wonder?

Our hearts and beliefs are a beautiful place to start exploring and experimenting to see your movement.

What do you believe? Why do you believe it? And how are you going go move about the world to make it so?

That's your movement.

That's the work you will show up to every day in every aspect—mundane and magickal—of your life.

That's what you, as an Artivist, came here to do.

VI. The Artivist: How To Change The World

"I change myself; I change the world." Gloria Anzaldua

As we reach into ourselves for honest, real, representational expressions of our experiences, something truly magical starts to happen.

Through doing the work of Radical Personal Alchemy—where we own our experiences and create from our marginalization and Otherness—to empower ourselves as Artivists, our art becomes not only infused and representational of our own stories, plights, and overcomings, but it also begins to tap into the Collectives.

When we share from a place of our truth, honesty, movement, and values *and* we empower and infuse those sharings with our experiences, the stories we tell, and the art we share, we begin to blur the lines between You and Me, Me and Us, and I and We. And our stories and art begin to weave, mesh, and alchemize into the Other.

Soon, folxs searching for representation of themselves in narratives of possibility, in the sea of white-washed art, manifesting, and magick dialogues, and in solutions of empowerment and justice for all begin to see a shimmer of themselves in your work and art.

That is the promise, hope, and revolution of The Artivist's work.

Not only do folxs begin to see themselves witnessed and reflected, but that mirror image looking back at them ignites a wave of heat in *their* belly as thoughts, sensations, and uncharted beliefs of "*If they can do it; so can i*" begin to ember.

That ember is the inkling that calls us to move from disenchantment to some kind of action that sparks change. That jolt of change is the very same spark mentioned in The Artivist's Call section at the top of this manifesto.

Only this time that spark wasn't ignited by me. That spark was ignited by *you. Through your art, your Artivism, you have inspired someone else to begin their journey and exploration of their own artivism.*

Because through our expression of our Otherness as our power and our turning it into powerful art, we become the ripple in the high and low tides of life.

And an ocean full of ripples become rip tides, tsunamis, and currents of ever ebbing and flowing, cleansing, life-giving, altering, and albeit sometimes destructive, waves of change.

But sometimes, we *do* have to burn it all down in order for all of us to be reborn from the ashes. *No one is free until all of us are free.*

Sometimes, we need to build a bridge between two worlds—one that does not always feel like it's worth saving and one that always is. *Art is the bridge.*

Sometimes, all we need, really and truly, *is* love. *And a little fairy dust of faith and a sprinkle of hope.*

But/and/also/all sometimes the only thing that will save us *is* our anger channeled and funneled into powerful art that offers up innovative solutions of change. *Our artivism.*

And you, as The Artivist.

The fire and medicine you carry?

We need all of it.

More potently, we need the medicine that rising and arting together brings—commonality, multiplicity, more expansibility.

We, like Earth who is home to *all* species and also houses *all* the energy of creation and death in a singular drop of water, were created and designed to embody all of life.

We were created to be and contain multitudes. And somewhere in that multitudeness is something as small as a pinhead or as large as a mountain that connects us. We can't always see it, but it's omnipresent and always there.

We are more alike than we are different. More interconnected than separate.

More equal than less than.

Only our humxness split the we, into me, into I.

Animals have co-existed on and with this planet and each other for *eons*. We can't even do it for the 10 minutes we spend on Facebook, Instagram, or anywhere else we hang out online.

Here's the truth The Artivist and their/our art usher in: There is, nor ever will be, a singular solution to a multi-dimensional problem, and we, as beings, will never be as one-dimensional and dichotomous as those in control and the systems they create demand us to be.

We are not boxes to be checked, but the pen that wanders off in the margins and writes something else entirely. That scribbles in an answer—our answer— that wasn't given as a choice.

We *always have choice.*

We are *always in agency.*

And so, my beautiful gente of Artivists, Healers, Magick-makers, Creatrixes, Liberators, and Medicine Keepers, you ask, **how do we change the world?**

We change the world by starting where we are.

By acknowledging our inner spark to create change and releasing any doubt that one person can make a difference.

We listen, honor, and follow our intuition—the intuitive hits, inklings, and sensations in our bellies.

We take action.

We follow the path with heart.

We express ourselves.

We find outlets to channel that expression and vision into solutions.

We take to the streets.

We pick up a microphone or a pen. We create art.

We write our way back to justice by turning our experiences into art.

And then we do it all on purpose.

Sound familiar? It should. Because it's the *exact same journey you took yourself through in this manifesto*—and i took myself through to first *become* The Artivist and then write about it.

All change, like art and life, is a cycle unto itself.

And the way we change the world *is* the exact same way we change ourselves into Artivists, into magick-

makers, into visionaries, rappers, writers, healers—
whatever we want to be.

Because one does not change without the other.

As below, so above. As above, so below. As within, so
without.

And so you create, write, riff, dance, paint, sing,
collage, speak your art solutions into being.

Thus creating the change you wish to see by being an
expression of it *first*.

There is really only one praxis left to do—it's the
forever one.

Keep doing what you are doing.

Keep being *The Artivist*.

By continuing to do so, you become part of our
Artivist story.

And the change you wish to see.

VII. The Artivist's Call To Action
Your Final Praxis

Because it is my life mission to get our voices out there, i have created a space on my website where i will be showcasing any and all work—however big or small—that this book inspires you to create. Please email your revolutionary art with links to *artivist@wokemagic.com*.

i am with you marching, chanting, praying, taking to the streets, and arting right alongside you.

Here's to our ever-expanding, ever-evolving creative visions for ourselves and the world.

With all the love, radicalization, and agency this Universe has to offer, i love you. And i bow in deep and never-ending gratitude for going on this journey with me.

Thank you for being a part of the solution.

And creating your art as part of our (r)evolution—for the highest good of all involved, ourselves included.

As we speak, create, art; so shall it be.

And so it is.

Thank you. Thank you. Thank you.

in lak'ech
xo-b

The Artivist: Further Exploration/ Resources

Please note that this is by no means an exhaustive list. It is a living document and list that we, as Artivists and documentarians of our plight, will continue to add to. If you know of someone you'd like to see referenced here, please email me at artivist@wokemagic.com and i will include them in future editions.

Thank you for contributing to the movement.

Artivists

Childish Gambino/Donald Glover - *Atlanta, Mr. & Mrs. Smith, This Is America*
i really believe his entire body of work is one big love note to, and as, The Artivist.

Gloria Anzaldúa - *this bridge called my back & many other revolutionary literary works*
This book was my introduction to Gloria and intersectionality. Every contributor in this anthology is an Artivist whose expression has something to teach. This book is a treasure trove of what artivism feels like.

Viktor Frankl - *Man's Search for Meaning*
i think about this book anytime i find myself feeling overwhelmed by the weight of systemic oppression and our fight as a people. This book is a call and chant to remember our power in every and all situation we find ourselves in—even the direst,

destitute, and oppressive, holds the seedling of personal agency; if we choose to see it that way.

N.W.A - *Their whole careers*
This is who i think of when i say the word, Artivist— *and they were doing it from the jump.* 2015's *Straight Outta Compton* bio pic is an excellent unfolding of what the essence of Artivism is about.

Frida - *Her life + art*
Whenever i think about transmuting pain into art, my mind immediately goes to Frida. Her bus accident was a gateway to her gift and the birth of her artistic and painting voice. And while she alchemized her pain and fragmentation on canvas, her body was a living legacy of lineage of the Mexican culture and people, and her house was a home for dissenters. Every piece of her life was woven with The Artivist's mission and heart.

*

As far as artivism goes, it's extremely important to me to share examples of folxs who aren't well known or famous so that we can all see what is possible for us.

Below are the Artivists who have been the most impactful to my own work.

Asha Frost - *You are the Medicine*
Asha is an Indigenous Healer and Medicine Woman and her work is a testament that Artivism can come in many forms. The most important form is the one

that looks like us. Artivism can be subtle, feminine (non-gendered), and deeply rooted in one's lineage and ancestry.

She is a beautiful example of what is possible when you come from a deep and rooted sense of who you are and where you come from—and own it in your art.

Her art was the key i needed to help uncork my reconnection to my own Indigenous roots and relate to Artivism in new, expanded ways.

See: *Dear White Woman Who Wants To Be Like Me* in her book, *You Are The Medicine*

Website: ashafrost.com   Insta: @ashafrost

Kayla Hamilton - *Circle O (Formally K Hamilton Projects)*

Kayla is a black, disabled dancer, educator, and founder of *Circle O* in The Bronx, NY. Her work sits at the intersections of disability, blackness, accessibility, and movement. Her concerts, movement pieces, choreography, and company are on the leading edge of making dance accessible to *all* folxs. As an Artivist, Kayla's work seeks to be (and is) representational of many marginalizations in the world of dance.

i met Kayla as an undergrad, where she was very much the exact same Artivist as she is today.

Website: circleo.org   Facebook: facebook.com/
CircleO.org

Mētztli Wolf - *Revolutionary Mystic and Black Moon Wolfdog Sanctuary*

Mētztli Wolf weaves the work of the mystic and activism into their land of Revolutionary Mystic. They have an online shop with candles that range from *Hex the Patriarchy* to *Liberated World* to *Witches Against White Supremacy*, literally fusing magick and activism together. But it was in their public dream of creating a Wolf Sanctuary that i was most called to. i write about their story in my book, *Magick For Transformation: Rituals and alchemy for manifesting your wildest dreams.*

As someone who has always wanted to have an animal sanctuary, Mētztli became proof of what was possible *for me.* Mētztli has taught me how to dream big. Not just dream big but how to call in and on community care to be an ally in our dream making and manifesting.

Website: revolutionarymystic.com
Patreon: patreon.com/revolutionarymystic
Insta: revolutionary_mystic

Chani Nicholas - *Chani App*

Chani has radicalized astrology in a way that makes the stars accessible and part of narratives of equality, justice, and self-care as activism. i think of her app as astrology for revolutionaries and Artivists. Her, the app, and books are all woven with the fabric of congruence—as in she lives, hires, and praxises the solutions she translates from the stars.

i have been an astrology student of Chani's since 2014 and the alchemy of activism and astrology was the proof i needed to begin to unravel how my magick, art, craft, and activism intersect *in a public career-facing way.*

Website: chaninicholas.com   Insta: @chaninicholas
App: app.chani.com/

More from me. *One Minute Sparks For Artivists.*

i created and launched this podcast a month *before* i received the original download for this book. The podcast was inspired by Alexandra Franzen's *Tiny Project* newsletter series, and the first episode was released on August 9, 2019 and ran for two seasons. i've collected all the episodes in one convenient place for you. Head over to www.brandiamaraskyy.com/theartivist to listen.

Books & Articles to assist you on your Artivist journey

These are some of the books and articles that have helped me understand, grow, and live into my own personal blend of Artivism. i share them in the Spellcast that they do the same for you.

Borderlands/La Frontera: The New Mestiza by Gloria E. Anzaldúa

This Bridge Called My Back: Writings by Radical Women of Color edited by Cherríe Moraga and Gloria E. Anzaldúa

this bridge called home: radical visions for transformations edited by Gloria E. Anzaldúa and Analouise Keating

pedagogy of the oppressed by Paulo Freire

Teaching to Transgress: Education As The Practice of Freedom by bell hooks

Red Tarot: A Decolonial Guide to Divinatory Literacy by Christopher Marmolejo

Create Dangerously: The Immigrant Artist At Work by Edwidge Danticat

Steal This Book by Abbie Hoffman

The War of Art: Break Through the Blocks and Win Your Inner Creative Battles by Stephen Pressfield

Man's Search For Meaning (i really cannot share this book enough) by Viktor Frankl

Making Art During Fascism by Beth Pinkens

Other books i haven't read but are on my to-be-read shelf:

Revolutionary Witchcraft: A Guide To Magical Activism by Sarah Lyons

Rest Is Resistance: A Manifesto by Tricia Hersey

Pleasure Activism: The Politics of Feeling Good by adrienne maree brown

Referenced in this manifesto

"The act of making art exposes a society to itself." Julia Cameron in her book *The Artist's Way.*

"Blood Memories" Alvin Ailey as quoted in this article: https://www.kennedy-center.org/education/resources-for-educators/classroom-resources/media-and-interactives/media/dance/alvin-ailey--revelations/#:~:text=Ailey%20described%20the%20memories%20that,that%20ran%20through%20his%20veins.

"Perfectionism is the voice of the oppressor, the enemy of the people." Anne Lamott in her book *Bird by Bird.*

"I change myself; I change the world." Gloria E. Anzaldúa in her book *La Frontera: The New Mestiza*

"By redeeming your most painful experiences you transform them into something valuable, algo para compartir or share with others so they too may be empowered." Gloria E. Anzaldúa in her essay "now let us shift . . . the path of conocimiento . . . inner work, public acts" in the book *this bridge we call home.*

Word Artivism

As Artivist we build the path as we go.

And language is a mirror. Our words create worlds.

But in order to do that, we must be able to understand and speak a common tongue.

It is in this spirit of community word world building that i share the following understandings of words and expressions as they came to me along the way in the hopes of creating a collective Artivist tongue.

Personal Agency - Found first in the *Caution* chapter in the book's opening. There are no epistemological origins of this word for me—only somatic. It's one of those phrases that i felt first and then turned to language to help me describe what i was feeling. *Personal agency* is the closest word i could unearth to describe the original, unequivocal, unshakable source of power that resides in us.

Personal agency is the center from which our power of choice emanates. It is the same force that animates the Universe and the world around us but within a humxn-born context and concept.

Personal agency is our power to choose. It's a stronger, more interconnected frequency than free will. Free will is what happens when we claim and exert our personal agency.

Personal agency is the key to our liberation, freedom, and transformation.

Ourstory - Found first in Part I, Section 1: *Spark*. Used as an all-inclusive, gender-neutral substitution for the word "history" or "herstory." In the end, this is OUR collective, all-species inclusive STORY.

Mapas - Found in Part II. i was first introduced to this term by fellow performance Artivist Volcano Del X. They used this term in reference to being a parent. It's a beautiful soliloquy of Mamma and Pappa and a beautiful example of how transformative the innovation of language (and parenting) can be.

Artivist - Found in the title and throughout this manifesto. When this word combination of art + activism came to me back in the early 2000s, i really believed i had made it up. But upon research, i noticed a few others and one website (artivism.com) using the term.

And now i understand it as a term for and by ALL of us. Those who live it. Those who create by it. Those who call it into their orbit.

An Artivist is someone who uses their art and/or expression as a vehicle and tool for societal, political, systemic, personal, global, and macro/micro change.

Artivist is less about the label/term than the action behind it.

As future praxis work, i deeply encourage you to make up your own definition through the experiences and living of your life of it.

(And come back and email me what you find!)

Acknowledgments

The biggest lie told about art and art-making is that one does it alone. We are never alone—even when it feels like we are. We all carry within us pieces and parts of our personal mentors and models who influence us; various chapters, stages, and incantations of ourselves; and the spirit of the land we reside on.

These are the spirit and folxs that i carry with me.

My ancestor's land.
It is my utmost honor and privilege to have sourced, channeled, and shared this book as a steward of the lands of my people, the Indigenous Mexicos known as modern-day Tejas. It was the winds of my ancestor's spirit and soul-voice threaded in my tongue, braided in my heart, and woven into the fabric of this book that encouraged me to finish it.

My teachers.
All who have bravely chosen to go first. They each paved a path for me to find the soul behind the work, the medicine on the page, and therefore myself, and art in my activism. They have given so much to the world and me; may i always be a reflection of the world they are/were creating their art to build.

My father.
For showing me that while Artivism may look, vote, express, and be called different for everyone, its soul is still the same—a soul of service. In service to

something greater than the self, more powerful than money, more potent than ego. It is through and amid our contrasting beliefs and values that i have learned how to expand my heart and vision so much that i can now see and feel how it all fits together. You have always been a gateway to expansion for me. May my words and work be an ever-revolving return of the favor.

My mother.
My original Artivist model. She showed me how, through simply living life in alignment and congruency with love, you can radically change someone else's. You have taught me the medicine + magic of the everyday Artivist and the greatest artivism there is—love. i am a literal living, breathing expression of your love. Thank you for showing me how to thread my love into everything i create, do, and say.

My grandmothers.
Whose medicine runs through me even though my logic tries to tell me it's too late. Thank you for paving the way.

My friends, believers, and supporters.
Dana. B. A. And every soul who has come into my orbit, chosen to stay, or leave. Thank you for being a part of my evolution. Your belief plays such a big part in my creation story. May i always be and do the same for you.

C.
You are the piece i never knew i needed, but the piece i had always been searching for. For the words, worlds, and portals you have opened up within and without me, thank you. All these channels, all these creations, all these words are always and foremost in resounding gratitude and love for you.

Myself.
For doing the work. For being vulnerable. For sitting at the desk for hours and hours upon end to birth this manifesto into physical reality.

And for the all the incantations of me the drafts upon drafts this manifesto has seen.

Brandi, You are worthy. You are enough. You are loved.

And you are already the change you so desperately ache to be. i love you. And i thank all you. 🙏

About the Author

Brandi Amara Skyy (she/they/we/us) is a Poet, Author, Wild Dream Witch; and founder of The Wild Dream Journal Club who believes we all have a fire and Universe inside waiting to Big Bang its way out of us.

They are the author of 8 books, including *The Little Book of Drag* (2022) and *Be More Drag* (2023) both published by Dog n Bone Books, *Magick For Transformation* (2024) published by Cico Books, and her latest work—a manifesto on using your art as activism called, *The Artivist.* Their work has been featured in BET, Curve Magazine, Global Grind, and Ofrenda Magazine (her first piece for BET went viral); and as a journalist, op-ed writer, TV anchor, and columnist for The Dallas Voice.

She grew up under the South Texas Sun, rhinestone beaches, and full familia tamale-making kitchen table wisdom. As a double Leo, they have been everything performative under the Sun: Junior Olympic artistic roller-skating champion, cross-country touring belly dancer, and award-winning drag queen.

Known as the "Queen of Firsts," they were the first to publish books on female drag queens and spearhead the first haute drag magazine, GAG Magazine; have their neo-drag performance group open up for Lady Gaga; and win the first National Drag Pageant, Miss Diva USofA in 2014.

As an Artivist, Brandi has been using her art as activism since 2005; has spoken on diversity inclusion to international companies like Southwest Airlines; lobbied Congress on behalf of the Human Rights Campaign while interning at the Women's Institute of Public Policy and Research in Washington DC; and has marched, led, and help organzine many street marches. They hold a BA in Dance and an MA in Multicultural Women's & Gender Studies from Texas Woman's University.

When they're not busy being the change they wish to see, Brandi can be found deepening her creative and magickal craft, on a cruise ship in the middle of the ocean, and/or obsessing over all things Lisa Frank and Dallas Cowboys football.

Brandi resides on her native lands, known as Wimberley, Tejas, with her wife Candace, and their spoiled, papaleta Maltese/Shih-Tzu rescue, June. For more about Brandi and living your Wild Dream Life head over to her Wild Dreamer Substack community, brandiamaraskyy.com, or YouTube & Instagram @brandiamaraskyy.

They are currently working on their 9th book, a memoir about the yearning for our lives to mean something.

One last thing ...

Believe and show up.

To your work.

To your mission.

To your art.

To yourself.

These two things—belief in your own power and showing up—are more valuable than money, then having access to high-end resources, or being 'classically trained.' All the tools, all the advice, all the books, teachers, lessons, and money in the world won't do you any good if you don't possess—and tend—to these two things within yourself.

Because belief paired with action is THE most important piece of progress, of creating change.

A few years ago, i saw a video of a New Orleans freestyle street performer, Ray Wimley, that went viral because Common jumped in to freestyle with him. (See video here: https://www.youtube.com/watch?v=4jcKywvtTNw)

What blew me away was not that Common joined in and made him famous, but had that not happened, Ray still would have shown up and kept playing anyway—because that's what he had been doing.

Common says in the description of his video that he saw Ray "a few years" *before he joined in*—meaning that Ray was showing up to the mic and the streets to make his art for *years* before that viral video moment happened.

What kept Ray going?

Belief in himself and his art paired with real-world action behind it.

Ray knew what he was doing was art and he showed up to it each and every day—regardless of who was watching and who believed/valued what he did as art.

And then one day, Ray's art spirit spoke and moved Common's. Common caught their freestyle on film and now Ray is living his dream and making his art. (You can find him @ray_wimley, The Freestyle Savant on Instagram).

And the rest is ourstory.

You have that same power to show up too.

WE ALL DO.

And it's my belief that, besides yourself which is first and foremost the most important, you just need *one other person* to believe in you.

And if you can't find that one person for yourself or don't believe they are out there, know that I BELIEVE IN YOU.

i believe in your power, your creativity, and the potency of your divine miraculous magick and ability to be proof of what is possible.

You've got this.

Go forth and be the change.

i believe in you.

i love you.

"The future started yesterday, and we're already late."
— John Legend
in his song, *If You're Out There*